THE PYTHON BIBLE

VOLUME FIVE

FINANCE

BY

F*LORIAN* D*EDOV*

Copyright © 2019

Copyright © 2019 Florian Dedov

Florian Dedov, Vienna

1st Edition

ASIN E-Book: B07WJW31B2

ISBN-10 Paperback: 1686407378

ISBN-13 Paperback: 978-1686407376

All rights reserved. No part of this work may be reproduced or transmitted in any form or by any means, electronic or mechanical, including photocopying, recording, or by any information storage or retrieval system, without the prior written permission of the copyright owner and the publisher.

TABLE OF CONTENT

Introduction
1 – Installing Modules
   Pandas
   Pandas-Datareader
   Matplotlib
   MPL-Finance
   Numpy
   Scikit-Learn
   Beautifulsoup4
   Installation
2 – Loading Financial Data
   Reading Individual Values
   Saving and Loading Data
      CSV
      Excel
      HTML
      JSON
      Loading Data From Files
3 – Graphical Visualization
   Plotting Diagrams
   Plotting Style
   Comparing Stocks
4 – Candlestick Charts
   Preparing The Data

- Plotting The Data
- The Candlestick
- Plotting Multiple Days
- 5 – Analysis and Statistics
  - 100 Day Moving Average
    - Nan-Values
  - Visualization
  - Additional Key Statistics
    - Percentage Change
    - High Low Percentage
- 6 – S&P 500 Index
  - Webscraping
  - Extracting The Data
  - Serializing Tickers
  - Loading Share Prices
  - Compiling Data
  - Visualizing Data
  - Correlations
    - Visualizing Correlations
- 7 – Trendlines
- 8 – Predicting Share Prices
- What's Next?

INTRODUCTION

Who wants to build long-term wealth needs to invest his capital. But nowadays investing isn't done in the same way as it was a couple of decades ago. Nowadays everything works with computers, algorithms, data science and machine learning. We already know that Python is the lingua franca of these fields.

In the last volumes we learned a lot about data science and machine learning but we didn't apply these to anything from the real world except for some public datasets for demonstration. This book will focus on applying data science and machine learning onto financial data. We are going to load stock data, visualize it, analyze it and also predict share prices.

Notice however that finance and investing always involves risk and you should be very careful with what you are doing. I am not taking any responsibility for what you are doing with your money. In this book we are only going to talk about the financial analysis with Python.

After reading this book you will be able to apply the advanced Python knowledge and the machine learning expertise that you've already got to the finance industry. Take time while reading this book and code along. You will learn much more that way. I wish you a lot of fun and success with this fifth volume.

Just one little thing before we start. This book was written for you, so that you can get as much value as possible and learn to code effectively. If you find this book valuable or you think you have learned something new, please write a quick review on Amazon. It is completely free and takes about one minute. But it helps me produce more high quality books, which you can benefit from.

Thank you!

If you are interested in free educational content about programming and machine learning, check out: https://www.neuralnine.com/

1 – Installing Modules

For this book we are going to use some libraries we already know from the previous volumes but also some new ones. We will need the following list:

- Pandas
- Pandas-Datareader
- Matplotlib
- MPL-Finance
- NumPy
- Scikit-Learn
- Beautifulsoup4

Now let's take a look at the individual libraries. We will recap the ones we already know and also explain what we will use the new ones for.

Pandas

Pandas is a library that we have already used in the past two volumes. It offers us the powerful data structure named data frame. With Pandas we can manage our data in a similar way to SQL tables or Excel sheets.

PANDAS-DATAREADER

The *Pandas-Datareader* is an additional library which we are going to use, in order to load financial data from the internet. It loads data from APIs into data frames.

MATPLOTLIB

Matplotlib is a library that we use to visualize our data and our models. We can choose from a variety of different plotting types and styles.

MPL-FINANCE

MPL-Finance is a library that works together with Matplotlib and allows us to use special visualization for finance. We will use it for plotting candlestick charts.

NUMPY

NumPy is our fundamental module for linear algebra and dealing with arrays. It is necessary for Matplotlib, Pandas and Scikit-Learn.

SCIKIT-LEARN

Scikit-Learn is the module that we have used in the last volume of The Python Bible series. It offers us a lot of different classic and traditional machine learning models. We are going to apply these models to our financial data in order to make predictions.

BEAUTIFULSOUP4

Last but not least, we are using a new module with the name *beautifulsoup4*. I admit that this is a pretty stupid and misleading name but this library is a powerful web scraping library. We are going to use it in order to extract financial data out of HTML files.

INSTALLATION

These are the installation commands (with pip) for the necessary libraries:

```
pip install pandas

pip install pandas-datareader

pip install matplotlib

pip install mpl-finance

pip install scikit-learn

pip install beautifulsoup4
```

2 – Loading Financial Data

Now that we have installed the necessary libraries we are going to start by taking a look at how to load financial data into our script. For this, we will need the following imports:

```
from pandas_datareader import data as web
import datetime as dt
```

We are importing the *data* module of the *pandas_datareader* library with the alias *web*. This module will be used to get our data from the Yahoo Finance API. Also, we are importing the *datetime* module so that we can specify time frames. To do that, we use the *datetime* function.

```
start = dt.datetime(2017,1,1)
end = dt.datetime(2019,1,1)
```

Here we have defined a start date and an end date. This is our timeframe. When we load the data, we want all entries from the 1st of January 2017 up until the 1st of January 2019. Alternatively, we could also use the *datetime.now* function, to specify the present as the end date.

```
end = dt.datetime.now()
```

The next step is to define a data frame and to load the financial data into it. For this we need to know four things. First: The ticker symbol of the stock we want to analyze. Second: The name of the API we want to receive the data from. And last: The start and end date.

```
df = web.DataReader('AAPL', 'yahoo', start, end)
```

We are creating an instance of *DataReader* and we pass the four parameters. In this case, we are using the Yahoo Finance API, in order to get the financial data of the company Apple (AAPL) from start date to end date.

To now view our downloaded data, we can print a couple of entries.

	High	Low	...	Volume	Adj Close
Date			...		
2017-01-03	116.330002	114.760002	...	28781900.0	111.286987
2017-01-04	116.510002	115.750000	...	21118100.0	111.162437
2017-01-05	116.860001	115.809998	...	22193600.0	111.727715
2017-01-06	118.160004	116.470001	...	31751900.0	112.973305
2017-01-09	119.430000	117.940002	...	33561900.0	114.008080

Warning: Sometimes the Yahoo Finance API won't respond and you will get an exception. In this case, your code is not the problem and you can solve the problem by waiting a bit and trying again.

As you can see, we now have a data frame with all the entries from start date to end date. Notice that we have multiple columns here and not only the closing share price of the respective day. Let's take a quick look at the individual columns and their meaning.

Open: That's the share price the stock had when the markets opened that day.

Close: That's the share price the stock had when the markets closed that day.

High: That's the highest share price that the stock had that day.

Low: That's the lowest share price that the stock had that day.

Volume: Amount of shares that changed hands that day.

Adj. Close: The adjusted close value that takes things like stock splits into consideration.

READING INDIVIDUAL VALUES

Since our data is stored in a Pandas data frame, we can use the indexing we already know, to get individual values. For example, we could only print the closing values.

```
print(df['Close'])
```

Also, we can go ahead and print the closing value of a specific date that we are interested in. This is possible because the date is our index column.

```
print(df['Close']['2017-02-14'])
```

But we could also use simple indexing to access certain positions.

```
print(df['Close'][5])
```

Here we would print the closing price of the fifth entry.

SAVING AND LOADING DATA

With Pandas we can now save the financial data into a file so that we don't have to request it from the API every time we run our script. This just costs time and resources. For this we can use a bunch of different formats.

CSV

As we have already done in the previous volumes, we can save our Pandas data frame into a CSV file.

```
df.to_csv('apple.csv')
```

This data can then be viewed by using an ordinary text editor or a spreadsheet application. The default setting is to separate the entries by commas. We can change that by specifying a separator in case our values contain commas.

```
df.to_csv('apple.csv', sep=";")
```

Here we would separate our data by semi-colons.

EXCEL

If we want to put our data into an Excel sheet, we can use the *to_excel* function.

```
df.to_excel('apple.xlsx')
```

When we open that file in Excel, it looks like this:

	A	B	C	D	E	F	G
1	Date	Open	High	Low	Close	Adj Close	Volume
2	2017-01-03 0:00:00	115.8	116.33	114.76	116.15	112.14	28781900
3	2017-01-04 0:00:00	115.85	116.51	115.75	116.02	112.0145	21118100
4	2017-01-05 0:00:00	115.92	116.86	115.81	116.61	112.5841	22193600
5	2017-01-06 0:00:00	116.78	118.16	116.47	117.91	113.8392	31751900
6	2017-01-09 0:00:00	117.95	119.43	117.94	118.99	114.882	33561900
7	2017-01-10 0:00:00	118.77	119.38	118.3	119.11	114.9978	24462100
8	2017-01-11 0:00:00	118.74	119.93	118.6	119.75	115.6157	27588600
9	2017-01-12 0:00:00	118.9	119.3	118.21	119.25	115.133	27086200
10	2017-01-13 0:00:00	119.11	119.62	118.81	119.04	114.9302	26111900
11	2017-01-17 0:00:00	118.34	120.24	118.22	120	115.8571	34439800

We can now analyze it further in the spreadsheet application.

HTML

If for some reason we need our data to be shown in browsers, we can also export them into HTML files.

```
df.to_html('apple.html')
```

The result is a simple HTML table.

JSON

Finally, if we are working with JavaScript or just want to save the data into that format, we can use JSON. For this, we use the *to_json* function.

```
df.to_json('apple.json')
```

LOADING DATA FROM FILES

For every file format we also have a respective loading or reading function. Sometimes we will find data in HTML format, sometimes in JSON format. With pandas we can read in the data easily.

```
df = pd.read_csv("apple.csv", sep=";")
df = pd.read_excel("apple.xlsx")
df = pd.read_html("apple.html")
df = pd.read_json("apple.json")
```

3 – Graphical Visualization

Even though tables are nice and useful, we want to visualize our financial data, in order to get a better overview. We want to look at the development of the share price. For this, we will need Matplotlib.

```
import matplotlib.pyplot as plt
```

Plotting Diagrams

Actually plotting our share price curve with Pandas and Matplotlib is very simple. Since Pandas builds on top of Matplotlib, we can just select the column we are interested in and apply the *plot* method.

```
df['Adj Close'].plot()
plt.show()
```

The results are amazing. Since the date is the index of our data frame, Matplotlib uses it for the x-axis. The y-values are then our adjusted close values.

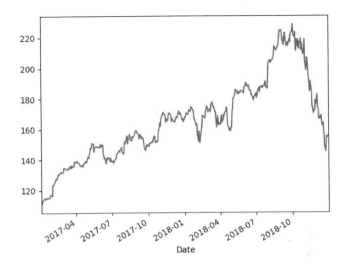

As you can see, with just two lines of code we plotted the two-year development of the Apple share price.

PLOTTING STYLE

Now we can improve the style of our plot. For this, let's start by choosing a style. At the following page you can take a look at the different pre-defined Matplotlib styles.

Styles: https://bit.ly/2OSCTdm

But before we can apply one, we will need to import the *style* module from Matplotlib.

```
from matplotlib import style
```

For our case, *ggplot* is probably the best suited style. It has a grid, nice colors and it looks smooth.

```
style.use('ggplot')
```

The next thing is our labeling. Whereas our x-axis is already labeled, our y-axis isn't and we are also missing a title.

```
plt.ylabel('Adjusted Close')
plt.title('AAPL Share Price')
```

Let's take a look at our graph now.

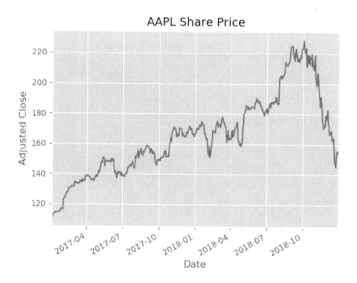

This looks much better. It is now way easier to understand what these values mean. However, there is a much better way to plot financial data. But this will be the topic of the next chapter.

Comparing Stocks

As we already know, we can plot multiple graphs into one figure. We can use this in order to compare the share price development of two companies.

```
style.use('ggplot')

start = dt.datetime(2017,1,1)
end = dt.datetime(2019,1,1)

apple = web.DataReader('AAPL', 'yahoo', start, end)
facebook = web.DataReader('FB', 'yahoo', start, end)

apple['Adj Close'].plot(label="AAPL")
facebook['Adj Close'].plot(label="FB")
plt.ylabel('Adjusted Close')
plt.title('Share Price')
plt.legend(loc='upper left')
plt.show()
```

Here we load the financial data of Apple into one data frame and the data of Facebook into another one. We then plot both curves. Notice that we are specifying a *label*, which is important for the legend that helps us to distinguish between the two companies. By using the *legend* function, we can activate the legend and specify its location. The result looks like this:

It looks pretty good. The problem here is that this only works because the share prices are quite similar here. If we would compare Apple to a company like Amazon or Alphabet, which shares cost around 1000 to 2000 dollars each, the graph wouldn't give us much information. In that case, we could work with subplots.

```
apple = web.DataReader('AAPL', 'yahoo', start, end)
amazon = web.DataReader('AMZN', 'yahoo', start, end)

plt.subplot(211)
apple['Adj Close'].plot(color='blue')
plt.ylabel('Adjusted Close')
plt.title('AAPL Share Price')

plt.subplot(212)
amazon['Adj Close'].plot()
plt.ylabel('Adjusted Close')
plt.title('AMZN Share Price')

plt.tight_layout()
plt.show()
```

What we do here is creating two subplots below each other instead of plotting the two graphs into one plot. We define a subplot for Apple and one for Amazon. Then we label them and at the end we use the *tight_layout* function, to make things prettier. This is what we end up with:

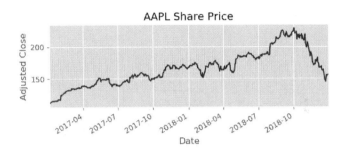

Now even though the share prices are radically different, we can compare the development of the two stocks by looking at the two graphs.

4 – Candlestick Charts

The best way to visualize stock data is to use so-called *candlestick charts*. This type of chart gives us information about four different values at the same time, namely the high, the low, the open and the close value. In order to plot candlestick charts, we will need to import a function of the MPL-Finance library.

```
from mpl_finance import candlestick_ohlc
```

We are importing the *candlestick_ohlc* function. Notice that there also exists a *candlestick_ochl* function that takes in the data in a different order.

Also, for our candlestick chart, we will need a different date format provided by Matplotlib. Therefore, we need to import the respective module as well. We give it the alias *mdates*.

```
import matplotlib.dates as mdates
```

Preparing The Data

Now in order to plot our stock data, we need to select the four columns in the right order.

```
apple = apple[['Open','High','Low','Close']]
```

Now, we have our columns in the right order but there is still a problem. Our date doesn't have the right format and since it is the index, we cannot manipulate it. Therefore, we need to reset the index and then convert our *datetime* to a number.

```
apple.reset_index(inplace=True)
apple['Date'] =
apple['Date'].map(mdates.date2num)
```

For this, we use the *reset_index* function so that we can manipulate our *Date* column. Notice that we are using the *inplace* parameter to replace the data frame by the new one. After that, we map the *date2num* function of the *matplotlib.dates* module on all of our values. That converts our dates into numbers that we can work with.

PLOTTING THE DATA

Now we can start plotting our graph. For this, we just define a subplot (because we need to pass one to our function) and call our *candlestick_ohlc* function.

```
ax = plt.subplot()
candlestick_ohlc(ax, apple.values,
                 width=5,
                 colordown='r',
colorup='g')
ax.grid()
ax.xaxis_date()
plt.show()
```

Besides the subplot, we are also passing a couple of other parameters here. First of all, our four financial values. We access these by referring to the *values* attribute of our data frame. Additionally, we define the width of the individual candlesticks and the colors for upward movements and downward movements. Last but not least, we turn on the grid and we define the x-axis as the date axis and our numerical values get displayed as dates again. This is our result:

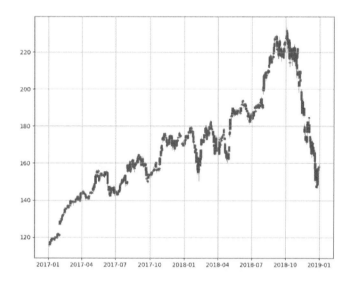

This might look a bit confusing right now but don't worry we will take care about that in a minute.

THE CANDLESTICK

First of all, we need to understand what a candlestick is and how it works.

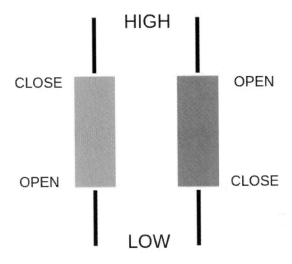

As you can see, we have two types of candlesticks – the green one and the red one. If the share price went up on that particular day, the candlestick is green. Otherwise it is red.

One candlestick gives us the information about all four values of one specific day. The highest point of the stick is the *high* and the lowest point is the *low* of that day. The colored area is the difference between the *open* and the *close* price. If the stick is green, the close value is at the top and the open value at the bottom, since the close must be higher than the open. If it is red, it is the other way around.

PLOTTING MULTIPLE DAYS

Another thing that we can do with this kind of plot is to plot the open, high, low and close of multiple days. For this, we can take one value like the *adjusted close* and calculate the four values for a specific amount of time.

```
apple = web.DataReader('AAPL', 'yahoo', start, end)
apple_ohlc = apple['Adj Close'].resample('10D').ohlc()

apple_ohlc.reset_index(inplace=True)
apple_ohlc['Date'] =
apple_ohlc['Date'].map(mdates.date2num)
```

By using the *resample* function we stack the data in a specific time interval. In this case, we take ten days (10D). At the end we apply the *ohlc* function, to get the four values out of our entries. Then we again have to convert our date into a numerical format.

Additionally, we are going to create a second subplot this time, which displays the volume for these days.

```
apple_volume =
apple['Volume'].resample('10D').sum()
```

This time however we are using the *sum* function, since we don't want to plot another candlestick chart but only the volume of these ten days.

Now we need to define the two subplots. For this, we are using the function *subplot2grid* which makes it easier to align the plots.

```
ax1 = plt.subplot2grid((6,1),(0,0),
                        rowspan=4,
colspan=1)
ax2 = plt.subplot2grid((6,1),(4,0),
                        rowspan=2,
colspan=1,
                        sharex=ax1)
ax1.xaxis_date()
```

The first tuple here (6,1) states the amount of rows and columns of the window. Here we define six rows and one column. The second tuple defines at which point the subplots start. The first one takes row one and column one, whereas the second one takes row four and column one. The parameters *rowspan* and *colspan* define across how many rows and columns our plots shall stretch. Also notice that we define that both subplots share the x-axis.

```
candlestick_ohlc(ax1, apple_ohlc.values, width=5,
                colorup='g', colordown='r')
ax2.fill_between(apple_volume.index.map(mdates.date2num),
                apple_volume.values)

plt.tight_layout()
plt.show()
```

We again just use the same function to plot our candlestick charts but this time we use our ten day values. Also, we plot our volumes on the second subplot by using the *fill_between* function. This creates a type of chart that fills the area below the graph. Our x-values here are the converted dates and our y-values are the volumes. This is the result:

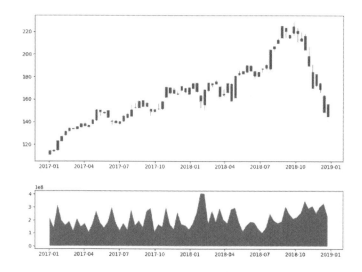

Since we only have one tenth the amount of values now, things are way more readable. We can see how the share price develops in a ten day interval.

5 – ANALYSIS AND STATISTICS

Now let's get a little bit deeper into the numbers here and away from the visual. From our data we can derive some statistical values that will help us to analyze it.

100 DAY MOVING AVERAGE

For this chapter, we are going to derive the *100 day moving average*. It is the arithmetic mean of all the values of the past 100 days. Of course this is not the only key statistic that we can derive, but it is the one we are going to use now. You can play around with other functions as well.

What we are going to do with this value is to include it into our data frame and to compare it with the share price of that day.

For this, we will first need to create a new column. Pandas does this automatically when we assign values to a column name. This means that we don't have to explicitly define that we are creating a new column.

```
apple['100d_ma'] = apple['Adj Close'].rolling(window = 100, min_periods = 0).mean()
```

Here we define a new column with the name *100d_ma*. We now fill this column with the mean values of every 100 entries. The *rolling* function stacks a specific amount of entries, in order to make a statistical calculation possible. The *window* parameter is the one which defines how many entries we are going to stack. But there is also the *min_periods* parameter. This one defines how many entries we need to have as a minimum in order to perform the calculation. This is relevant because the first entries of our data frame won't have a hundred previous to them. By setting this value to zero we start the calculations already with the first number, even if there is not a single previous value. This has the effect that the first value will be just the first number, the second one will be the mean of the first two numbers and so on, until we get to a hundred values.

By using the *mean* function, we are obviously calculating the arithmetic mean. However, we can use a bunch of other functions like *max, min* or *median* if we like to.

NaN-Values

In case we choose another value than zero for our *min_periods* parameter, we will end up with a couple of *NaN-Values*. These are *not a number* values and they are useless. Therefore, we would want to delete the entries that have such values.

```
apple.dropna(inplace=True)
```

We do this by using the *dropna* function. If we would have had any entries with *NaN* values in any column, they would now have been deleted. We can take a quick look at our data frame columns.

```
print(apple.head())
```

	High	Low	...	Adj Close	100d_ma
Date			...		
2017-01-03	116.330002	114.760002	...	111.286987	111.286987
2017-01-04	116.510002	115.750000	...	111.162437	111.224712
2017-01-05	116.860001	115.809998	...	111.727715	111.392380
2017-01-06	118.160004	116.470001	...	112.973305	111.787611
2017-01-09	119.430000	117.940002	...	114.008080	112.231705

VISUALIZATION

To make this statistic more readable and in order to compare it to our actual share prices, we are going to visualize them. Additionally, we are also going to plot our volumes again. This means that we will end up with an overview of the share price compared to our 100 day moving average and of how many shares changed their owners. For this, we will again use two subplots.

```
ax1 = plt.subplot2grid((6,1),(0,0),
                        rowspan=4, colspan=1)
ax2 = plt.subplot2grid((6,1),(4,0),
                        rowspan=2, colspan=1,
                        sharex=ax1)
```

Again we use the same proportions here. Our main plot will take up two thirds of the window and our volume plot will take up one third. Now we just need to plot the values on the axes.

```
ax1.plot(apple.index, apple['Adj Close'])
ax1.plot(apple.index, apple['100d_ma'])
ax2.fill_between(apple.index,
apple['Volume'])

plt.tight_layout()
plt.show()
```

The result is a very nice overview over price, volume and our statistical value.

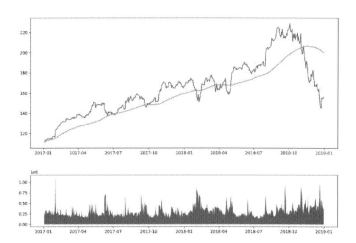

ADDITIONAL KEY STATISTICS

Of course there are a lot of other statistical values that we can calculate. This chapter was focusing on the way of implementation. However, let us take a quick look at two other statistical values.

Percentage Change

One value that we can calculate is the percentage change of that day. This means by how many percent the share price increased or decreased that day.

```
apple['PCT_Change'] = (apple['Close'] - apple['Open']) / apple['Open']
```

The calculation is quite simple. We create a new column with the name *PCT_Change* and the values are just the difference of the closing and opening values divided by the opening values. Since the open value is the beginning value of that day, we take it as a basis. We could also multiply the result by 100 to get the actual percentage.

High Low Percentage

Another interesting statistic is the high low percentage. Here we just calculate the difference between the highest and the lowest value and divide it by the closing value. By doing that we can get a feeling of how volatile the stock is.

```
apple['HL_PCT'] = (apple['High'] - apple['Low']) / apple['Close']
```

These statistical values can be used with many others to get a lot of valuable information about specific stocks. This improves the decision making.

6 – S&P 500 Index

When we talk about how the markets are doing, we are usually looking at indices. One of the most important indices is the so-called *S&P 500* index which measures the stock performance of the 500 largest companies listed on the US stock exchanges.

Up until now, we always downloaded financial data for individual stocks from the internet. But when we are doing larger calculations many times, it would be preferable to not need to bother the Yahoo Finance API every time.

For this reason, we can download the stock data of the 500 companies which are represented in the S&P 500 right now and save them into files. We can then use these files instead of making requests to the API all the time.

Webscraping

The Yahoo Finance API doesn't offer any possibilities to request all the companies of the S&P 500 index. Therefore, we will need to get the information about which companies are represented from somewhere else. And for this, we will need something called *webscraping*.

With webscraping we are reading the HTML files of a website, in order to extract some specific information we are looking for. In this case, we are going to use the Wikipedia page of the list of S&P 500 companies to get the information we need.

Link:
https://en.wikipedia.org/wiki/List_of_S%26P_500_companies

On this page, we can find a table with all the 500 companies and different information about them. We can see the name of the company, the industry, the headquarters location and some more things. What we need however is the ticker symbol, which we can find in the first column (make sure you take a look at the page yourself, since the structure of the table might change from time to time).

To now understand how we can extract the information out of this website, we need to look at the HTML code. For this, we go into our browser, make a right click and view the source code of the page.

```
<table class="wikitable sortable" id="constituents">

<tbody><tr>
<th><a href="/wiki/Symbol" title="Symbol">Symbol</a>
</th>
<th>Security</th>
<th><a href="/wiki/SEC_filing" title="SEC filing">SEC f
<th><a href="/wiki/Global_Industry_Classification_Stand
<th>GICS Sub Industry</th>
<th>Headquarters Location</th>
<th>Date first added</th>
<th><a href="/wiki/Central_Index_Key" title="Central In
<th>Founded
</th></tr>
<tr>
```

There we can see a *table* with table rows (*tr*) and within these rows we have table data (*td*). So we can find a way to filter the elements.

Extracting The Data

For webscraping with Python we will need the library *beautifulsoup4*, which we installed in the beginning of this book. Also, we will need the library *requests*, which is built-in into Core-Python. We will use requests to make HTML requests and beautifulsoup4 to extract data out of the responses.

```python
import bs4 as bs
import requests
```

First we need to get the HTML code into our program. For this, we make a request.

```python
link = 'https://en.wikipedia.org/wiki/List_of_S%26P_500_companies'
response = requests.get(link)
```

We use the *get* function to make a HTTP request to the website and it returns a response which we save into a variable.

Now we need to create a *soup object*, in order to parse the content of the response.

```python
soup = bs.BeautifulSoup(response.text, 'lxml')
```

We use the *BeautifulSoup* constructor to create a new soup object. As the first parameter we pass the *text* attribute of the response. The second parameter defines the parser that we choose. In this case, we pick *lxml* which is the default choice. However, it may be the case that it is not installed on your computer. Then you just need to install it using pip as always.

When we have done that, we define a *table* object which filters the HTML file and returns only the table we are looking for.

```
table = soup.find('table', {'class': 'wikitable sortable'})
```

We use the *find* function of our soup object to find a *table* element. Also, we pass a dictionary with the requirements. In this case, we want a table, which has the classes *wikitable* and *sortable*.

```
<table class="wikitable sortable" id="constituents">
```

If you want to exclude other tables on this side, you can also define the *id* if you want.

What we now do is creating an empty list for our ticker symbols. We then fill this list with the entries from the table.

```
for row in table.findAll('tr')[1:]:
    ticker = row.findAll('td')[0].text[:-1]
    tickers.append(ticker)
```

By using the *findAll* method we get all elements which are a table row. We then select every element except for the first one, since it is the header. Then we use the same function to get all the table data elements of the first column (index zero). Notice that we are using the [:-1] notation here to cut of the last two letters, since they contain a new line escape character. Finally, we save our tickers into our array.

To make our script more readable and modular let's put all of our code into a function.

```python
def load_sp500_tickers():

    link = 'https://en.wikipedia.org/wiki/List_of_S%26P_500_companies'
    response = requests.get(link)

    soup = bs.BeautifulSoup(response.text, 'lxml')

    table = soup.find('table', {'class': 'wikitable sortable'})

    tickers = []

    for row in table.findAll('tr')[1:]:
        ticker = row.findAll('td')[0].text[:-1]
        tickers.append(ticker)

    return tickers
```

Now we have our code in a function, which we can call whenever we need it. This is useful because we are going to extend our program a bit further.

SERIALIZING TICKERS

So that we do not have to scrape our ticker list over and over again, we will save it locally and then read it out whenever we need it. We do that by serializing IT. During serialization, we save an object, including the current state, in a file. Then we can reload it in exactly that state whenever we want. For the serialization, we use pickle, which we know from previous volumes.

```python
import pickle
```

We now add two lines to our function before the return statement. These are responsible for serializing the ticker object.

```python
with open("sp500tickers.pickle", 'wb') as f:
    pickle.dump(tickers, f)
```

Now when we scrape our tickers from the Wikipedia page once, we can save them in a file, to reload them whenever we want. But since the list is changing from time to time, we might have to update it.

LOADING SHARE PRICES

Up until now we only have the ticker symbols and nothing more. But of course we want all the financial data as well. So now we are going to download the stock data for each ticker symbol from the Yahoo Finance API. This will take up a couple of hundred megabytes (depending on the time frame). But first we will need three additional imports.

```python
import os
import datetime as dt
import pandas_datareader as web
```

The *datetime* and the *pandas_datareader* module should be obvious here. But we are also importing the *os* library which provides us with basic functions of the operating system. We will use it for directory operations.

Now we are going to create a second function for loading the actual share prices. We start by getting our ticker symbols into the function.

```python
def load_prices(reload_tickers=False):

    if reload_tickers:
        tickers = load_sp500_tickers()
    else:
        if os.path.exists('sp500tickers.pickle'):
            with open('sp500tickers.pickle', 'rb') as f:
                tickers = pickle.load(f)
```

Here we have the function *load_prices*. It has one parameter which's default is *False*. This parameter decides if we are going to scrape the tickers anew or if we are going to load them from our serialized file. If we want to scrape it again, we call our first function. Otherwise we check if our pickle file exists and if yes we load it. You can also define an else-tree which defines what happens when it doesn't exist. Maybe you want to also call the first function in that case.

The next thing we need to do is to create a directory for our files. We will create a CSV file for every single ticker symbol and for these files we want a new directory.

```python
if not os.path.exists('companies'):
    os.makedirs('companies')
```

We again use the function *os.path.exists* to check if a directory named *companies* exists (you can choose any name you like). If it doesn't exist, we use the *makedirs* method to create it.

Now let's get to the essence of the function, which is the downloading of our data.

```
start = dt.datetime(2016,1,1)
end = dt.datetime(2019,1,1)

for ticker in tickers:
  if not os.path.exists('companies/{}.csv'.format(ticker)):
    print("{} is loading...".format(ticker))
    df = web.DataReader(ticker, 'yahoo', start, end)
    df.to_csv('companies/{}.csv'.format(ticker))
  else:
    print("{} already downloaded!".format(ticker))
```

Here we defined a pretty narrow time frame. Three years are not enough for a decent analysis. However, you can adjust these values as you want but the broader your time frame, the more time it will take and the more space you will need.

Basically, what this function does is just checking if a CSV file for a specific ticker symbol already exists and if it doesn't it downloads and saves it.

Now when you run this script and it starts downloading, you may notice that it takes quite a while. One interesting idea would be to implement a faster way to download the data using multithreading and queues. This would be a nice exercise for you. If you need some help for doing this, check out the second volume, which is for intermediates.

COMPILING DATA

All good things come in threes. Therefore we are going to write a third and last function that compiles our data. We will take the data out of each of the 500 CSV files and combine it into one data frame. Then we will export that data frame into a new final CSV file.

Let's start by loading the ticker symbols into our function.

```python
with open('sp500tickers.pickle', 'rb') as f:
    tickers = pickle.load(f)

main_df = pd.DataFrame()
```

As you can see, we create a new empty data frame here. This *main_df* will be our main data frame which contains all values. We are now going to extract the *adjusted close* value from every CSV file and add this column to our main data frame. This means that in the end, we will have a CSV file with the adjusted close value for all companies.

```python
print("Compiling data...")
for ticker in tickers:
  df = pd.read_csv('companies/{}.csv'.format(ticker))
  df.set_index('Date', inplace=True)

  df.rename(columns = {'Adj Close': ticker}, inplace=True)
  df.drop(['Open', 'High', 'Low', 'Close'], 1, inplace=True)

  if main_df.empty:
    main_df = df
  else:
    main_df = main_df.join(df, how='outer')
```

Here we have a for loop that iterates over all ticker symbols. For every ticker symbol we load the respective CSV file into a data frame. Then we set the index of this data frame to be the *Date* column, since we will need a common index. We then rename the *Adj Close* column to the ticker symbol. This is because we will have one big CSV files with 500 columns and they should not all have the same name. Then we drop all the other columns except for *Date*. Last but not least we check if our main data frame is empty or not. If it is empty, our first data frame becomes the main data frame. Otherwise, we join the data frame onto our main data frame using an outer join. We've discussed joins in previous volumes.

```
main_df.to_csv('sp500_data.csv')
print("Data compiled!")
```

At the end we save our main data frame into a new CSV file and we're done. We can now run our functions.

```
load_prices(reload_tickers=True)
compile_data()
```

VISUALIZING DATA

Now we have a local CSV file with all the S & P 500 Index tickers. So, for a while, we don't need to ask the Yahoo Finance API for past data.

```
sp500 = pd.read_csv('sp500_data.csv')
sp500['MSFT'].plot()
plt.show()
```

We load our CSV file into a DataFrame and can then, simply indicate our desired ticker symbol in the square brackets. In this case, we draw the graph of Microsoft.

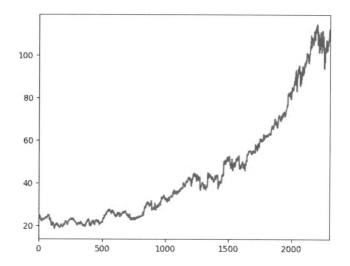

CORRELATIONS

Finally, for this chapter, let's look at a very interesting feature of Panda's data frames. This function is called *corr* and stands for *correlation*.

```
correlation = sp500.corr()
```

Here we create a correlation data frame, which contains the values of the correlations between individual share prices. In a nutshell this means that we can see how the prices influence each other.

```
print(correlation)
```

	MMM	ABT	ABBV
MMM	1.000000	0.919446	0.928664
ABT	0.919446	1.000000	0.907837
ABBV	0.928664	0.907837	1.000000
ABMD	0.812892	0.888733	0.888560
ACN	0.963421	0.952070	0.936506

The numbers we see here show us how "similar" the change in the prices of the individual stocks is. The stocks MMM and MMM have a correlation of 100% because they are the same stock. On the other hand, ABBV and MMM have only about 93% correlation, which is still a lot.

If you look at the whole table, you will find that there are some correlations that are less than 1% and even some that are negative. This means that if stock A falls, stock B rises and vice versa. They are indirectly proportional.

VISUALIZING CORRELATIONS

This table can be very helpful in analyzing and predicting prices. We can also visualize the correlations using a special Matplotlib function.

```
plt.matshow(correlation)
plt.show()
```

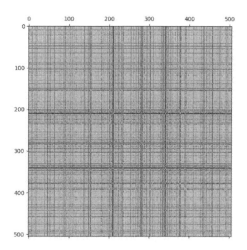

You can use the Matplotlib window to zoom into the correlations. The more yellow a point is, the higher the correlation.

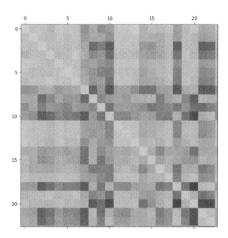

This is quite a nice way to visualize correlations between share prices of different companies.

7 – REGRESSION LINES

In this chapter, we are going to use linear regression in order to plot regression lines. These indicate in which direction the share price is going in a specific time frame. For this chapter we are going to need NumPy.

```
import numpy as np
```

First, we are going to load our financial data again.

```
start = dt.datetime(2016,1,1)
end = dt.datetime(2019,1,1)

apple = web.DataReader('AAPL','yahoo', start, end)
data = apple['Adj Close']
```

In this case, we again choose the company Apple. As a next step, we need to quantify our dates in order to be able to use them as x-values for our algorithm. The y-value will be the adjusted close.

```
x = data.index.map(mdates.date2num)
```

Here we again use the function *date2num* and we map it onto our *Date* column. The next step is to use NumPy to create a linear regression line that fits our share price curve.

```
fit = np.polyfit(x, data.values, 1)
fit1d = np.poly1d(fit)
```

You will notice that this implementation of linear regression is quite different from the one, we already used in the last volume with scikit-learn. Here we use

NumPy. First we call the *polyfit* method to fit a model for the x-values (our dates) and the y-values (the prices). The last parameter (one) is the degree of the function. In this case, it is linear. What this function returns to us is a list of coefficients. To now use this list and make an actual function of it, we need the second method *poly1d*. It takes the list and constructs a function for *x*. So our variable *fit1d* is actually a callable function.

We can now use what we have in order to plot our share price graph and the regression line for it.

```
plt.grid()
plt.plot(data.index, data.values, 'b')
plt.plot(data.index, fit1d(x),'r')
plt.show()
```

First we just plot our price graph in blue color. Then we plot our regression line. Here our x-values are also the dates but the y-values are the result of our *fit1d* function for all input values, which are our numerical dates. The result looks like this:

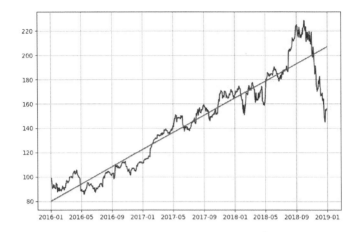

Now we just need to be able to choose the time frame for which we want to draw the regression line.

SETTING THE TIME FRAME

So first we need to define two dates in between of which we want to draw the regression line. We do this as always with the *datetime* module.

```
rstart = dt.datetime(2018, 7, 1)
rend = dt.datetime(2019, 1, 1)
```

In this case, we want to look at the six months from the 1st of June 2018 to the 1st of January 2019. What we now need to do may be a bit confusing. We will create a new data frame and cut off all other entries.

```
fit_data = data.reset_index()
pos1 = fit_data[fit_data.Date >=
rstart].index[0]
pos2 = fit_data[fit_data.Date <= rend].index[-1]

fit_data = fit_data.iloc[pos1:pos2]
```

Here we create the data frame *fit_data* which starts by copying our original data frame and resetting its index. Then we calculate two positions by querying data from our new data frame. We are looking for the first position (index zero) in our data frame, where the *Date* column has a value greater or equal to our start date. Then we are looking for the last position (index negative one) where our *Date* column has a value less or equal to our end date. Finally, we cut out all other entries from our data frame by slicing it from position one to position two.

Now we of course need to rewrite our *fit* functions a little bit.

```
dates = fit_data.Date.map(mdates.date2num)

fit = np.polyfit(dates, fit_data['Adj
Close'], 1)
fit1d = np.poly1d(fit)
```

We again create a new variable *dates* which contains the dates from our time frame in numerical format. Then we fit the regression model with our data again.

```
plt.grid()
plt.plot(data.index, data.values, 'b')
plt.plot(fit_data.Date, fit1d(dates),'r')
plt.show()
```

At the end, we again plot our two graphs. But this time we refer to the *Date* column specifically since it is no longer the index of the *fit_data* data frame. This is the result:

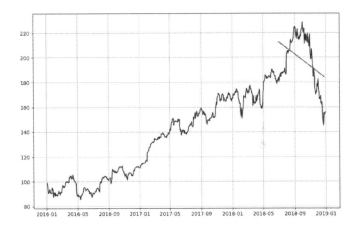

This time we can clearly see that the slope is negative, since the prices go down in that time frame.

8 – Predicting Share Prices

Now in this last chapter, we will use machine learning to predict our share price development. However, this prediction won't be reliable, since it is quite simplistic and it is generally very hard to predict the markets. This is more about learning how to apply machine learning to financial data. For this chapter, we will need the following libraries in addition to the ones we already used:

```
from sklearn import preprocessing
from sklearn.model_selection import train_test_split
from sklearn.linear_model import LinearRegression
```

You should be familiar with these from the previous volume. We have one library for preprocessing our data, one for splitting our data into training and testing data and one library which provides the machine learning algorithm itself.

Loading and Preparing Data

We are going to use linear regression again. But first, of course, we will need to load our data again.

```
start = dt.datetime(2016,1,1)
end = dt.datetime(2019,1,1)

apple = web.DataReader('AAPL','yahoo', start,
```

```
end)
data = apple['Adj Close']
```

Now how are we going to predict our share prices? Our approach will be quite simple. We are going to choose an amount of days and then shift our prices by that amount. Then we can look at the data and see how they have developed in past times and predict how they are going to do it in future times.

```
days = 50
data['Shifted'] = data['Adj Close'].shift(-days)
data.dropna(inplace=True)
```

Here we defined 50 days. We create a new column *Shifted* which contains our prices shifted upwards by 50 days using the *shift* function. At the end, we drop the *Nan* values which we have in this new column.

The next step is to prepare our data so that our model can learn from it. For this, we will need to convert it into NumPy arrays.

```
X = np.array(data.drop(['Shifted'],1))
Y = np.array(data['Shifted'])
X = preprocessing.scale(X)
```

Our x-value will be the adjusted close share price. For this, we drop the shifted column. As a y-value we choose only the shifted values. In order to make computations more efficient, we scale our x-values down. We normalize them.

Training and Testing

Now we are going to split our data into training data and into test data.

```
X_train, X_test, Y_train, Y_test =
train_test_split(X,Y,test_size=0.2)
```

We are using a test size of 20%, which means that we use 80% of the data for training and 20% for calculating the accuracy.

```
clf = LinearRegression()
clf.fit(X_train, Y_train)
accuracy = clf.score(X_test, Y_test)
print(accuracy)
```

We create a linear regression model and then fit it to our training data. After that we use the *score* method to calculate our accuracy.

```
0.8326191580805993
```

Most of the time the result will be around 85% which is actually not that bad for predicting share prices based on share prices.

Predicting Data

We can now use our trained model to make predictions for future prices. Notice however that this is not a tool or model that you should be using for real trading. It is not accurate enough.

```
X = X[:-days]
X_new = X[-days:]
```

Here we cut out the last 50 days and then create a new array *X_new* which takes the last 50 days of the remaining days. We will use these for predicting future values. For this, we will use the *predict* function of our model.

```
prediction = clf.predict(X_new)
print(prediction)
```

The results we get are our predicted prices for the next upcoming days:

```
[185.41161298 185.06584397 184.52124063 187.43442155 188.80890817
 190.08825219 190.66744184 190.21792733 188.69649258 188.29022104
 189.19786639 187.83204987 187.91852237 186.22418294 186.13775077
 183.50119313 184.20140126 183.30238569 182.8355713  180.4583505
 182.41201333 182.17861958 183.33694511 182.99983276 184.78920724
 181.97114204 183.25051294 185.4721155  187.72833126 187.52951038
 185.39433999 188.11731637 188.37665321 188.01359776 188.48038526
 187.57273991 188.85211081 188.47174204 188.61870362 189.82028557
 191.39357963 190.86626272 188.07410028 187.14914161 187.47763764
 197.16804184 202.25960924 202.77828293 203.71189826 202.01758572]
```

What's Next?

With this volume finished, you can consider yourself a very advanced Python programmer. You are able to write high level code and apply it to real-world problems and use cases. With the knowledge gained from this book, you can even develop your own portfolio analysis or management tool. You can use data science and machine learning to program your own financial software.

The skills you possess right now are crucial in today's economy. They are rare and very valuable. I encourage you to continue your journey. Even though you have already learned quite a lot, we don't stop here. There are a lot of topics to be covered yet and you should not miss out on them. Practice what you've learned, play around and experiment! I wish you a lot of success on your programming journey! Stay tuned and prepare for upcoming volumes.

Also, if you are interested in free educational content about programming and machine learning, check out https://www.neuralnine.com/

Last but not least, a little reminder. This book was written for you, so that you can get as much value as possible and learn to code effectively. If you find this book valuable or you think you learned something new, please write a quick review on Amazon. It is completely free and takes about one minute. But it helps me produce more high quality books, which you can benefit from.

Thank you!

NeuralNine

If you are interested in free educational content about programming and machine learning, check out https://www.neuralnine.com/

There we have free blog posts, videos and more for you! Also, you can follow the ***@neuralnine*** Instagram account for daily infographics about programming and AI!

Website: https://www.neuralnine.com/

Instagram: @neuralnine

YouTube: NeuralNine

Made in the USA
Columbia, SC
30 July 2020